Just Like That

A story of hope for a child's grief

Story by Chad A. Current

Illustrations by Jonathan Gibson

ISBN: 978-1-937602-07-9

Dust Jacket Press
PO Box 721243 Oklahoma City, OK 73172
www.DustJacket.com
Info@DustJacket.com
www.facebook.com/dustjacketllc
Follow us on Twitter at: DustJacketLLC

Illustration and Design: Jon Gibson

The Purpose of the Story

The purpose of this story is to help children process the death of a loved one. It is written from a Christian, biblical perspective, inviting children to imagine heaven. This story is also meant to help a child find a voice for the painful emotions he or she is feeling when confronted with loss. It is the prayerful hope of the author that *Just Like That* will serve as a tool adults can use to help children through the grief process.

The Story Behind the Story

Just Like That was inspired by the true story of the Wittung family. On January 10th, 2010, Jeff Wittung died from injuries he sustained in a car accident that occurred four days earlier, on his way to work. Jeff was only 35. He left behind a wonderful, faith-filled wife, Marne, and two beautiful little girls; five-year-old Ana, and one-year-old Kate.

Jeff had been my friend since we met at Mount Vernon Nazarene University in Mt. Vernon, Ohio. We were roommates at the Nazarene Theological Seminary in Kansas City, Missouri, where we each earned a Master of Divinity. At the time of his death, Jeff was pursuing his doctorate through Drew University and working for Baker Publishing Group in Grand Rapids, Michigan, and I was Lead Pastor at Living Hope Church of the Nazarene in Centerville, Ohio. Because of my history and friendship with Jeff, Marne asked me to come to the hospital and stand by his family as Jeff fought for his life. I arrived at the hospital just a few hours before Jeff transitioned from this life to his eternal life.

The day after Jeff's death, I prayed for what to say at the funeral, and this story began to flow from my heart and mind. And just like that, in a few hours I had finished the story. With Marne's blessing, I decided to share this story as the message for the funeral. I dedicated this story to the memory of Jeff and his faith in Christ. It was also my way to honor Marne, Ana, and Kate, whose faith in Christ is helping carry them through their devastating loss. At Marne's request, proceeds from the sale of this book will be committed to supporting a scholarship in Jeff's name at Mount Vernon Nazarene University.

Ana is only five years old but dares to think big thoughts. One night as she lay in bed she wondered, what's heaven like? She had wondered about heaven before but was more interested now than ever because her daddy, she'd been told, had gone there. She drifted off to sleep that night with thoughts of her daddy and with questions about heaven swirling around in her head.

Ana hadn't been asleep for long when she was awakened by a soft voice singing her name. "Aaaaaana," the voice sang sweetly. When Ana opened her eyes, a light (so bright it almost hurt her eyes!) filled her bedroom. It was like the sun was shining right there in the center of the room.

Once Ana's eyes adjusted, she could see a smiling woman, bathed in bright light, at the side of her bed. The woman had sparkling blue eyes and long, flowing blond hair that seemed to float around her.

Even though she didn't know who the woman was, Ana was not at all afraid. The bright, beautiful lady gently touched Ana's cheek as she spoke.

"Hello Ana," she said. "My name is Charity and I'm an angel. God sent me to answer your questions."

"He did?" Ana asked.

Not only was Ana unafraid of Charity, she also found that she didn't feel the least bit shy around the angel, the way she might with some people.

"There are many girls and boys who have the same questions as you, Ana," Charity said. "Many of their daddies have gone to heaven too. God wants me to answer your question so that you can help Him tell other children what heaven is like. Would that be okay with you?"

"Yes!" Ana squealed. "Are you really going to tell me about heaven?" she asked.

"Better than that," Charity answered. "I'm going to show you what heaven is like."

"Really?" Ana said excitedly. "But how can you do that?"

"Take my hand and I'll show you," Charity said smiling.

Ana squeezed Charity's hand, and just like that Ana's bedroom disappeared.

Ana looked around to see that she and Charity now stood on a magnificent hillside.

"Just like that," said Charity.

"Just like what?" asked Ana.

"Just like that -- from your bedroom to heaven," Charity said. "From Michigan to heaven -- just like that." But Ana had another question.

"What about a hospital? Can you go from a hospital room to heaven just like that too?"

"That's right," Charity answered. "Just like that, Jesus reached out his hand to your daddy, squeezed it tight, and just like that, your daddy went from a hospital room to heaven." [1]

Ana looked all around. Heaven was more beautiful than she could have imagined. The grass was greener than any green she had ever seen. It was so soft under her bare feet that it tickled when she walked. And when she took a step--Oh, what a surprise!--flowers bloomed all around her in bright whites and vivid reds, purples, and oranges.

"Every step in heaven blooms with life,"[2] Charity said.

Ana took another step and more flowers bloomed. When Ana finally understood, she began to jump and run through the grass, and with each step, more brightly-colored flowers bloomed around her. Ana giggled as she rolled around in the flowers. Charity giggled too. Ana liked that a lot.

Suddenly, Ana fell silent. Something off in the distance had caught her eye. "What's that?" she asked pointing.

Charity knelt down, put her cheek to Ana's, and whispered in her ear. "That is the Kingdom of God,"[3] she said.

"Wow! It's so bright and shiny," Ana said, looking closer. "But where is the sun? How can it be so bright with no sun?"

"Your daddy told us how smart you are and he was right," Charity said smiling. "There's no sun in heaven, but it's always day because Jesus is the light."[4] Ana liked the thought of that a lot.

"Charity?" Ana whispered.

"Go ahead, Ana," Charity said. "Ask me anything you want."

"Is that where my daddy is?"

Charity didn't respond with words but her answer was loud and clear. Charity danced. Oh, how she danced! She danced like there was music when there wasn't. She took Ana's hands and they danced together. They danced all over the hillside.

Somehow Ana knew this meant that her daddy was way over there, in the Kingdom of God. She realized then, that when you ask an angel if someone is in heaven and the person is there, the angels become so happy and excited that they can't answer with words, so instead they dance![5] Ana liked that a lot.

"Can we go to the Kingdom of God?" Ana asked. Charity reached out and took Ana by the hand again. Ana squeezed Charity's hand tight, and just like that they went from the hillside to the gates of the Kingdom of God.

"Do you remember what I told you, Ana?" Charity asked. Ana nodded.

"Just like that my daddy went from the hospital to heaven because he let Jesus hold his hand."

"That's right, Ana," Charity said. "You're every bit as smart as your daddy said."

"Have you talked to my daddy?" Ana asked.

"Of course. He's told us all about you," Charity said. "Your daddy will love you, your sister, Kate, and your mommy forever."

When Charity said that, Ana felt like someone hugged her even though no one was there.
Ana liked that a lot too.

"That gate is beautiful," Ana said in awe.[6] "It's so white that it shines.
Is that how you enter the Kingdom of God?"

"That gate is there to remind us of the real gate," Charity said. "The one, true gate; the only way anyone ever enters the Kingdom of God."

"What's that?" Ana asked.

"It's not a what," Charity explained. "It's a who." Then Charity bowed in worship as she pointed to Jesus beaming in His own light of love. "Jesus is the gate,[7]" she said. "A long time ago your daddy invited Jesus into his life, so when he died, Jesus invited your daddy to come into his home -- the Kingdom of God."

Ana was really excited now. "I've asked Jesus into my life," she beamed. "Does that mean I can go in too?"

"Someday," Charity said. "But not yet."

"When do I get to go in?" Ana asked.

"Only God the Father knows that,"[8] explained Charity.

This made Ana sad and she could feel tears welling up in her eyes. She wanted to see her daddy so much.

Charity could see the sadness in Ana's face. "You can't enter now," she said. "But from here you can listen. Close your eyes and tell me what you hear."

Ana closed her eyes tight and listened as carefully as she could. Then, to her delight, she heard it. "Music!" she said. "I hear music and laughing and--" She gasped. "I hear Daddy! And he's so happy!" Ana liked that most of all.

"There's someone else who has something to say to you," Charity said next.

Ana closed her eyes again, listened, and she did hear another voice. "I know that voice," Ana said. "But I don't know who it is."[9]

Charity smiled. "Yes, you know that voice," she said. "It's God the Father and he has a special message for you. A message he wants you to tell Kate when she is old enough to understand. It's a message that many others need to hear too. Listen, Ana."

And just like that, from that day on, God the Father held the hands of Ana, Kate and their mommy during their brightest days and their darkest nights. They knew that no matter what, they didn't have to be afraid. And whenever anyone would ask Ana how her family could be so brave, she would simply smile and say, "It's just like that."

Bible References Index

1. Luke 23:42-43; John 3:16-21; Revelation 3:20

2. Revelation 22:1-3

3. Revelation 21:1-4

4. Revelation 21:23-25; John 8:12 & 9:5; 1 John 1:5-7

5. Luke 15:1-10

6. Revelation 21:21

7. John 10:7-10

8. Matthew 24:36-51

9. John 10:1-5

10. Isaiah 41:10 (Jeff chose this as his verse to live by for 2010)

The purpose of this story is to help children process the death of a loved one. It is written from a Christian, biblical perspective, inviting children to imagine heaven. This story is also meant to help a child find a voice for the painful emotions he or she is feeling when confronted with loss. It is the prayerful hope of the author that Just Like That will serve as a tool adults can use to help children through the grief process.

About The Author

Chad Current is the son of Rick and Rose Current who showed him how real and personal God is. He is a graduate of Mount Vernon Nazarene University (BA in Religion) and Nazarene Theological Seminary (M. Div.). He is husband of Kimberly, who he is proud to say is way outside his league. He is the dad of Anna and Seth, who he loves with all his heart. He serves as the Lead Pastor of Living Hope Church which was started in 2000 and is a body of believers who are absolutely recklessly abandoned to being real, transformed, connected and poured out. He is a follower of Christ, who continually pushes him out of comfort and convenience through His amazing grace. To contact Chad visit www.elivinghope.com.

About The Illustrator

Jon Gibson serves as the Pastor of Creative Arts and Worship at Living Hope Church. He is on a lifelong journey of discovering creative and relevant ways to share the love of Jesus that has captivated is own heart! He is also the Head Designer Guy at Visual Artistries. He is a husband to Heather, the love of his life and dad of Morgan, Marlee & Mackenzie who are three of the most beautiful girls in the world! To contact Jon visit www.visualartistries.com. To check out more about Living Hope visit www.elivinghope.com.